SCHIRMER'S LIBRARY
OF MUSICAL CLASSICS

STEPHEN HELLER

Op. 47

Twenty-Five Studies

For the Piano

For Developing a Sense for
Musical Rhythm and Expression

Complete — Library Vol. 178

G. SCHIRMER, Inc.

DISTRIBUTED BY
HAL•LEONARD®
CORPORATION
7777 W. BLUEMOUND RD. P.O. BOX 13819 MILWAUKEE, WI 53213

PREFACE

Stephen Heller was born in Budapest on May 15, 1813. From a very early age he had begged his parents to let him take piano lessons. One day (as he later described in a letter to Robert Schumann) his father brought home half-a-dozen players from the local regimental band and said:

"Here, Stephen, I've brought you some people who understand this stuff; take your pick. The one you like best shall be your piano teacher."

One of these, a clarinettist, Bohemian by birth, proved satisfactory. Several weeks later the boy secretly wrote, in honor of his teacher, a set of variations on a Bohemian song. Here is his own description, written several years later, of its first performance:

"I had written almost everything Tutti—Violin, 'Cello, Flute, Bassoon, and Drums (I was seven years old). I'll never forget it! Imagine over a dozen players in a little room, with an audience consisting of the proud conductor of the regimental band in the seat of honor on the sofa, and a few of my teachers from school—and then the jumble of my composition! All my classmates . . . had been invited, since we did not have any music stands and they had to hold up the music for the players. Father ran around in seventh heaven."

After this triumph he was given lessons by the choirmaster in one of the big Budapest churches. Soon he made a public appearance at one of the local theaters, playing with his teacher a two-piano concerto by Dussek.

His father, perhaps too eager to make money out of his son's talents, sent him to Vienna, where he studied briefly under Karl Czerny, and then for a longer time under Anton Halm. Through Halm he met Beethoven and Schubert. Soon, at the age of thirteen, Heller was giving concerts in Vienna. And at the age of fifteen he was going on long concert tours through central Europe.

On these tours he met many of the great musicians of the world. One winter, at Warsaw, for example, he became acquainted with Chopin, and gave a concert jointly with Paganini.

But after five years of this life of a travelling concert artist—a period which he later spoke of as "five murderous years, a nomad life, restless, hopeless, aimless"—he found that he could not go on; though he was then only seventeen, he felt completely worn out. As he was at Augsburg when his concert tour thus reached a standstill, he remained at Augsburg for eight years, as teacher and as musician for Count Fugger, a nobleman whose family had long been active in the cultural life of that city. While there he began a correspondence with Robert Schumann, which ripened into a fine and lasting friendship between the two composers.

From Augsburg he went—at the advice of Friedrich Kalkbrenner—to Paris. Heller's first years in Paris were very hard. Kalkbrenner was to have been his teacher and mentor, but Heller—like Chopin—soon found that Kalkbrenner had nothing to teach him. For several years he supported himself by whatever arranging, teaching, and performing he could find to do. Being of a naturally retiring nature, he had a difficult struggle at first. But after about five or six years he became established; and the fact that he continued to live in Paris for almost fifty years (*i.e.*, until his death, on January 15, 1888) indicates the contentment and security that he found for himself there. During those Paris years he was in intimate contact with many of the leading musicians of Europe—Chopin, Berlioz, Halévy, Alkan, Panofka, David, Wolff, Seligman, and a whole group of musicians centering around Karl Hallé.

In the course of his long and fruitful life, Heller wrote several hundred piano pieces, classified under some 150 opus-numbers. Of these, the studies Op. 45-47 have particular vitality. They were written in 1844, six years after he had gone to Paris. They thus mark the time of his making a secure place for himself in that great city of music. They were written when he was at the height of his powers, a great pianist just entering his thirties—a young man, yet one who had already behind him extensive experience as a concert artist, teacher, and composer.

WILLIS WAGER

CONTENTS

Although the composer did not originally give these pieces descriptive titles, tradition has associated certain titles or ideas with certain of the numbers. In this table of contents they have all been assigned titles, which furnish a clue to the mood and musical thought of each study.

Twenty-five Studies

For developing a sense for musical rhythm and expression.
(Pour former au sentiment du rhythme et à l'expression.)

Allegretto. (♩ = 80.)

STEPHEN HELLER. Op. 47, Book 1.

1.

Allegretto con moto. (♩.=100.)

3.

Andante con moto (♩ = 108)

4.

Allegretto poco agitato. (♩ = 126.)

5.

perdendosi.

Vivace. ($\flat$.=108.)

7.

Allegro vivace. ($\dot{o} = 76$.)

8.

Andantino. ($= 69$.)

9.

D. C. ad lib.

10.

Moderato. (♩ = 100.)

Allegretto. (♩ = 126.)

13.

Twenty-five Studies

For developing a sense for musical rhythm and expression.

(Pour former au sentiment du rhythme et à l'expression.)

STEPHEN HELLER. Op.47, Book 2.

Allegretto con moto. (♩. = 80.)

14.

20.

Da Capo ad lib.

Andante con moto. ($\quad$= 84.)

21.

Allegro assai. ($\bullet$ = 138.)

22.

Allegretto con moto.(♩= 63.)

24.

Molto vivace.

Più vivo.

SCHIRMER'S LIBRARY
of Musical Classics

PIANO METHODS, STUDIES, AND EXERCISES
SERIES THREE

LOESCHHORN, A.

L. 1616	Op. 52.	20 Melodious Studies.
L. 966	Op. 65.	Studies for the development of Technique and Expression. Part I: For Beginners. Complete.
L. 310		The same: Bk. I.
L. 311		The same: Bk. II.
L. 312		The same: Bk. III.
L. 967	Op. 66.	The same: Part II: For the Intermediate Degree. Complete.
L. 968	Op. 67.	The same: Part III: For More Advanced Pupils. Complete.
L. 1615	Op. 169. 170.	Universal Piano Studies. For Medium Grade.
L. 254		Pianoforte Technics. Daily Exercises.

LÖW, J.

L. 913	Op. 281.	Octave-Studies.

MACFARREN, W.

L. 1037	Scale and Arpeggio Manual.

MENDELSSOHN, F.

L. 1523	3 Etudes from Op. 104; Scherzo à Capriccio.

MENOZZI, J.

L. 843	Metodo Teorico-Practico de Lectura Musical. sp. (Carrillo).

MOSCHELES, I.

L. 403	Op. 70.	24 Studies. Finishing Lessons for Advanced Performers. (Pauer). sp. e.
L. 404	Op. 70.	The same: Bk. I.

MOZKOWSKI, M.

L. 1798	Op. 72.	15 Etudes de Virtuosité.

NEUPERT, E.

L. 797	12 Studies.

NOLLET, E.

L. 1375	Op. 43.	15 Melodious Studies. (Hughes).

OESTERLE, L.

L. 1154	Instructive Course of Pieces. Bk. I: Elementary and Grade I. 48 Pieces.
L. 1155	Bk. II. Grade 2. 35 Pieces.
L. 1156	Bk. III. Grade 3. 25 Pieces.
L. 1157	Bk. IV. Grade 4. 22 Pieces.

PARLOW, E.

L. 1251	30 Little Etudes. Easy and Attractive Studies by Burgmuller, Czerny, Parlow, and others.

PHILLIP, I.

L. 1611	Op. 78.	6 Octave Studies in the Form of Little Fugues.
L. 1650		School of Octave-Playing. Bk. I: Exercises.
L. 1651		The same: Bk. II: 10 Original Studies by Alkan, Chopin, Czerny, Kessler, Kreutzer, Mathias, Mayer, de Mereaux, Wolff.

L. 1652	The same: Bk. III: Examples from Masterworks.
L. 1717	Elementary Rhythmic Exercises for the Five Fingers.
L. 1675	Exercises on the Black Keys.

PISCHNA, J.

L. 792	Technical Studies. 60 Progressive Exercises. (Wolff).

PLAIDY, L.

L. 304	Technical Studies. (Klauser). Complete.
L. 1617	The same: Bk. I.
L. 1618	The same: Bk. II.

RAVINA, H.

L. 1515	Op. 50.	Harmonious Etudes.

RUBINSTEIN, A.

L. 791	Op. 23.	6 Etudes. (Gallico).

SCHMITT, A.

L. 434	Op. 16.	Preparatory Exercises. Five-Finger Exercises (with Appendix by A. Knecht).

SCHULZ, F. A.

L. 392	Scales and Chords in all the Major and Minor Keys.

SCHUMANN, R.

L. 1727	Op. 3.	Studies after Paganini's Caprices and Op. 10 6 Concert Studies after Paganini's Caprices (Bauer).
L. 96	Op. 13.	12 Symphonic Studies. (Bauer).

SCHWALM, R.

L. 796	Daily Exercises.

SCHYTTE, L.

L. 1371	Op. 108.	25 Short and Melodious Studies.

SPANUTH, A.

L. 1579	Five-Finger Exercises.

STAMATY, C.

L. 1136	Op. 36.	Rhythmic Training for the Fingers. sp. e.
L. 858	Op. 37.	Singing Touch and Technique. 25 Easy Studies for Small Hands.

STREABOG, L.

L. 478	Op. 63.	12 Very Easy and Melodious Studies. First Degree.
L. 479	Op. 64.	The same: Second Degree.

TAUSIG, C.

L. 1353	Daily Studies (Ehrlich).

VOGT, J.

L. 965	Op. 145.	24 Octave-Studies of Medium Difficulty.

WIECK, F.

L. 66	Studies.

WOLFF, B.

L. 1099	Op. 118.	12 Short Octave-Studies.
L. 898		The Little Pischna. 48 Practice Pieces.

A-1175